Scroll Saw for Beginners

The Complete Hand Book to Craft 20 Beautiful Woodworking Scroll Saw Patterns and Projects with Tools and Tips Included

By

Jerry Heath

Copyright © 2021 – Jerry Heath

All rights reserved

No part of this publication may be reproduced, distributed, or transmitted in any form or by any means, including photocopying, recording, or other electronic or mechanical methods, without the prior written permission of the publisher, except in the case of brief quotations embodied in reviews and certain other non-commercial uses permitted by copyright law.

Disclaimer

This publication is designed to provide competent and reliable information regarding the subject matter covered. However, the views expressed in this publication are those of the author alone, and should not be taken as expert instruction or professional advice. The reader is responsible for his or her own actions.

The author hereby disclaims any responsibility or liability whatsoever that is incurred from the use or application of the contents of this publication by the purchaser or reader. The purchaser or reader is hereby responsible for his or her own actions.

Table of Contents

Introduction 7

Chapter 1 9

Basics of Saw Scrolling 9

    What is a Scroll Saw? 9

    The Evolution of Scroll Saw 11

    Common Types of Scroll Saw 16

        Parallel Arm 16
        C-Arm 17
        Double Parallel Link Arm 17
        Rigid Arm 17

    Benefits of the Scroll Saw 18

    Profiting From Saw Scrolling 18

Chapter 2 25

Saw Scrolling Tips and Tricks 25

Chapter 3 33

Getting Started with Saw Scrolling 33

    Tools and Supplies 33

- Wood 33
- Scroll Saw 36
- Scroll Saw Adhesives 42
- Clamps 46
- Drill Bits 47

Choosing the Right Scroll Saw Blade 49

Scroll Saw Safety Guidelines 52

Scroll Saw Essentials 54

How to Finish Scroll Saw Projects 57

Chapter 4 61

Saw Scrolling Projects 61

- Personalized Tree Plaque 61
- Botanical Trivets 63
- Wooden Utensil Trivet 66
- Rainbow Planter Sconce 68
- Wood and Macrame Plant Wall Hanger 74
- Scrolly Scalloped Mirror 77
- Circle Monogram Pallet Wood Décor 79
- Butterfly Silhouette Clock 83

Bracket-Shaped Barn Board Sign 87

State/Country Plaque 89

Mother's Day Plaque 91

Custom Corbels 94

Fall-Themed Monogram Wreaths 98

Wooden Paper Doll 101

Cutout Silhouette Plaques 105

Wooden Typography Artwork 108

Wooden Arrow Name Plaques 111

Wooden Logo Sign 115

Name Puzzle 118

Personalized Picture Plaque 121

Chapter 5 125

Fixing Common Saw Scrolling Problems 125

Chapter 6 136

Saw Scrolling Frequently Asked Questions (FAQs) 136

Conclusion 149

Introduction

Saw scrolling is one very unique craft. Although it is not so pronounced as other common crafts, this craft allows you to make many pretty highly-priced decorative pieces.

There are many types of saw used to work on materials like wood, ceramics and metals. Many of these saws are directly made to be used for this project and nothing else.

For instance, saws for wood can't be used on metals and the same goes for the others. You have to get a saw for everything you want to do. It is hard or impossible to come by a saw that can be used freely and intricately on multiple types of materials.

The scroll saw is a unique saw that can be used for several purposes. You can be rest assured that your woodwork, ceramics, metallic, and every form of work that requires sawing are covered.

It is a very simple tool that can be handled by anyone, even though it looks complicated. It can also be used to make very intricate and careful designs that no other instrument can achieve.

With just a scroll saw and other basic tools, you can craft a beautiful decorative piece.

If you are just starting, you might be wondering how hard it will be to master this tool and use it professionally. It is easy for anyone to learn how to use a scroll saw, as it is a little different from the other saws, but it is quite hard to master. There are many tricks and tips you need to get familiar with.

Hence, you must commit yourself to practice and intense learning if you are to become a pro in saw scrolling. The journey starts from learning and practicing. I am glad that you have begun yours by grabbing this book

Saw scrolling comes with much fun. It can be quite challenging and time taking, but it is still fun. I hope you have fun learning about this interesting craft.

Chapter 1

Basics of Saw Scrolling

What is a Scroll Saw?

The scroll saw is a small electric or pedal-operated saw that is used domestically and industrially to cut intricate and well-detailed curves in solid materials like wood or metals. It has a very fine and sharp blade than normal. The blades are made so that they can make a mark on any surface, no matter how hard the surface is.

The fineness of the blade is top-notch. Also, it can be used to make cuts other common saws like jigsaws cannot make.

The name scroll saw is derived from its traditional use in making scrollwork, and sculptural ornaments, which featured unique scroll-head designs.

It works with such rapidity and accuracy that it is very exciting, sometimes difficult to believe. It also reflects strength and flexibility when in use.

The scroll saw is made with a well-sharpened blade that is fixed in a vertical position in a suitable frame. The lathe's rotary action ensures it gains a reciprocating rectilinear motion from the lathe's rotary action. There is a conversion of line. This conversion of the line of motion is usually affected by contrivance, particularly deserving of notice from its extreme simplicity and cheapness.

Unlike the popular power saw which is used in making straight cuts across lumber with its rotating blades, scroll saws are used to make more complicated techniques like making puzzle pieces, wooden figurines, intarsia, and beveled edges.

Scroll saws have thin blades that slice in an up and down motion. This way, it is easy to follow the curves, bends, and complex patterns.

One more unique thing we need to appreciate about the scroll saw is its ability to make precise and intricate cuts or curves. The way you have imagined it to be, so will it appear.

They are also very versatile in use. You can carry them about.

The woodwork done with a scroll saw is known as ornate woodwork. This woodwork consists of a large variety of familiar kinds of works. Fretwork is done with a fretsaw. You will understand more about fretsaw in the next subhead.

Unlike the typical band saw that is known for having a continuous loop, a scrolling saw has a reciprocating blade. The scroll saw's blade is easily manipulated; it can be removed and placed through a pre-drilled starting hole without stress. The unique details of the blade and its varied tooth count permit significantly more intricate curves than the narrowest gauge band saw blade.

The majority of scroll saws offer a light, flexible arm and dust nuzzle blower to keep the workspace clean when working.

This is a tool made for those who create detailed work. It helps you to brew creativity while designing. The scroll saw is commonly used by woodworkers in designing. They bring woodworks to life.

The Evolution of Scroll Saw

Lack of accurate records would hinder us from having an in-depth insight into the inception and invention of scroll saw; where, when, and by whom it started. There is no comprehensive record of information covering details on the history of the scroll saw.

However, we have been graced with a little documentation that records the names of some prominent persons that contributed fully to the invention of this great tool.

Sawing delicate wooden shapes has been a common craft practice since the late 1500s. It began in Germany, where crafts were very much celebrated. It started during the reign of fretwork, the sawing of intricate shapes from wood. There are examples of fretwork –like decorations on early Egyptian, Greek, and Roman furniture. These designs and decorations are probably carved or cut with a blade knife.

Sawing of delicate wooden shapes wasn't popular until a German craftsman, also known as a clockmaker, developed a technique for making narrow and quite complex but yet, simple blades. This was around the 1500s.

Not too long after, a Parisian started to develop specialized hand tools for cutting intricate designs. He made his experiment of fretsaws and successfully designed a unique fretsaw that was U-shaped and originally known as a Buhl-saw; Buhl was a negative slang name given to him. It was found very interesting that he decided to name his design after his slang name.

This saw is very similar to the coping saw, one of the finest saw used for detailed work.

Mr. Boulle popularly addressed as Buhl gained notoriety in his work in a very short time. Unlike other conventional inventions that took time to be generally accepted in society. His craft was legitimized and quickly spread to Italy within a generation. His work is still popular today.

Soon after, Fretwork was introduced to America in the mid-1800s as Sorrento wood carving. The technique Sorrento was named so because it was invented in an area in Italy named Sorrento, where that type of carving was most popular. By the 1860s, the first mechanical fret saws called scrollsaws became popular amongst craftsmen in the US. This idea was incepted by a common craftsman who had the passion of using the thin blades on a reciprocating machine. He experimented and it was quite successful. Unfortunately, he remains nameless and it is not also known the reasons or circumstances that surrounded his invention.

The machine was patented in 1829. The patent is in the name of M'Duff, who people claim to be the early inventor, but a large number of persons share a different opinion; they acclaim that he happens to be just one of the inventors and not the main person.

Revisiting the register of arts and journal of patent inventions, it was discovered that on the Second of December 1829. M'Duff was awarded the Dr. Fellowees' Annual prize for the best machine invented by a working member of the London England Mechanic's institution, who couldn't make the award day.

During the ceremony, M'Duff was to perform with the tool, and it was realized that the tool was indeed one of its kind.

He made a great impression by using the scroll saw to cut America out of the Nigerian map carefully and rapidly.

Many people started experimenting with it, and from it, the great art of woodworking and metal sawing was invented. There are several models of scroll saws with unique blade sizes.

Many craftsmen started trying out their unique style of the scroll saw. The movement was so common, such that by 1857 there were more than three patents for improvements to the already patented scroll saw. Other patent references to American inventions were exhibited at crystal palace in London during the popular World Art Exhibition in 1851.

One of the unique inventions or modifications, as it were, was reported to have attached a rod to the wheel of a band saw to drive another blade to be used as a scroll saw.

By the 1860s, there were appearances of mechanical powered scroll saws using foot-powered treadles, a hand crank, or a pedal mechanism.

Thus, it can be said that scroll saw came from the lineage of fine narrow hands saws.

Within (1850 – 1910), which happened to be the Victoria era, scroll saws were popularly used to make cuts in ornamental pieces. Some of these cuts were mainly used to make designs on the surface rather than real deep designs. By this time, scroll saws were used to make delicate ornamental designs and creative patterns on roof eaves, furniture, and porches. It was also used to create and decorate simple clocks, common furniture, wall plaques, wooden frames, and other decorative pieces to adorn the home.

Not too long into the 1920s, the term scroll saw is now popularly used in America, and international manufacturer's organizations like New Rogers, Barners, Lester, Star, and hobbies.

Common Types of Scroll Saw

Scroll saw is usually classified according to the size of its throat. The throat area is generally identified as the distance from the location of the blade to the back end of the saw. The size or width of the throat determines the size of wood or material that it can work on.

Moderate saw sizes range from 12 inches (300 mm) to 30 inches (760 mm), depending on the brand and the size.

To cut really large wood or materials, the top mechanical linkage of the saw is usually hanged from a high position or the ceiling. This way, the saw would have an arbitrary deep throat. Aside from throat sizes, scroll saws are also categorized according to the arm type.

Parallel Arm

The original design of the parallel arm saw goes back to before 1870. This design contains two arms running parallel to each other with the blade attached to the ends of each arm. Two pivot points are majorly used in this design. This makes the saw's blade frequently move in a seemingly up and down motion. This is the only type of scroll saw that could do that; hence it is not out of place to term it the safest modern machine.

C-Arm

As you would rightly guess, this design has an arm shaped like a "C" with the sharp blade attached to the ends of the C curve. It has only one pivot point and creates a cut that is aggressive and in an arc. Unlike the parallel arm saw, if the blade breaks, the top portion of the blade continues to move up and down without stop until you finally shut off the saw with your hands.

Double Parallel Link Arm

This is the most recent design of the scroll saw. The blade is reliant on the two parallel arms that occasionally go back and forth. Thereafter, it converts this motion at all the tips of the two arms into an up and down blade motion.

Rigid Arm

This was a popular design in the Delta jigsaws of the '30s and '40s. Most recently, this design was featured in a tech company to model the production.

Benefits of the Scroll Saw
1. It allows for a substantial amount of creativity.
2. Scroll saw allows you to make amazing designs with just a penny. It does not require so many tools. Some saw scrolling projects require only the saw and some tools. You don't need to make so much investment in purchasing tools for use.
3. Scroll saws are used to cut intricate curves and joints. They are used to cut out shapes deeply and quickly and with accuracy.
4. They are used with modern intarsia.
5. They are very safe to use. Unlike conventional blades like the table saw, the harsh contact between the scroll saw blade and the fingers or limbs of the operator is unlikely to result in serious injury due to its smaller blade and relatively slower speed.
6. You can make money from it. It is a highly rewarding skill.

Profiting From Saw Scrolling

Nothing is as exciting as the possibility of turning passion to profit. Yeah, you might not be interested in learning this skill for money-making, but it is just interesting that you could just get paid to do what you love or what you find fun.

If you ask me, saw scrolling is a whole lot of fun and very exciting. Though it could be tiring, you are certain to have a nice time while working with the scroll saw. It is much more fun when this basic thing can grease your hand with money. Everyone would love that.

However, it is not as easy as it sounds. There are a lot of things that influence the level of profit an individual can make through saw scrolling. It is one thing to realize this, and it is another to overcome it and make it work. One of the most effective ways of selling is by showing people what you got, by selling your goods at a craft and art fairs where people will be looking out for unique and intricate work.

Here is a brief list of how you can make a profit from saw scrolling.

1. Home Décor
2. Furniture
3. Toys
4. Kitchen wear
5. Contracted work
6. Teaching scroll

1. Home Décor:

   The scroll saw is very skilled in making detailed imprints or cuts on materials; you can make intricate cuts with the scroll saw. This makes it a perfect tool for making home décor materials. Just like drawing, you can use the scroll saw to create unique curves and angles in both wood and metal that people can display in their homes. When this design is done on a larger piece of wood and hanged on the wall, they become the main highlight of the room. This is one of the most profitable and common saw scrolling projects ever. More sales from this are made than all others combined. Some of these interesting home décor ideas are wooden crosses, name plaques, monogrammed signs, holiday ornaments, wooden baskets, topography art, decorative boxes, clocks, and others.

2. Furniture:

   This is a vaster shelf of an idea of what you can use the scroll saw to make. Aside from making home decors, you can also use scroll saws on large pieces of furniture to make them more detailed and unique. There are some creative ways and techniques that can be applied using the scroll saw, like imprinting curves at the back of the chairs or decorative additions to legs for the tables, and shelf. Some many patterns and designs can be done on the surface of a material like wood or metal. This is why the scroll saw is very unique. It doesn't affect the shape or consistency of the material, it only designs it to give it a pleasurable or homely look. You can get designs or pattern ideas from searching through the art gallery or a website. Some persons love ornate furniture with lots of embellishments. A list of common furniture you can attempt saw scrolling are; children's furniture, wood-backed chairs, shelving, end tables, coffee tables, and many others. You could always innovate a pattern and do something you love. However, the children and baby's design is a booming niche that you can make a fortune from. It is even higher in demand.

3. Toys:
Wooden toys will always have that special value because it is well-made and pleasing to the eye. Also, wood allows for versatility. There are

children and adult's wooden toys. Some of them are wood puzzles, toy cars and trains, doll furniture, toy houses, figurines, etc.

These things are more durable when they are wooden or metal.

4. Kitchen Wear:
   A kitchen is a place where the magic happens and the dead are revived to being. Hence the apparatus in use must be carefully selected. Also, it won't be out of place to adorn the kitchen and give it a permanent facelift. It will help your magic start quickly and easily.

   Wood kitchen items are not just beautiful but practical and usable. They are easier to use and happen to be more practical in usage. If you prefer working with smaller items on the scroll saw, look into decorative kitchen items that will allow you to try out your creativity. It will be enjoyable to make and bring glamour to your kitchen. Tools by which you can experiment with your creativity are trivets, cutting boards, napkin holders, wooden utensils like salad forks, and large serving spoons, baskets, and others.

5. Contracted Work:

   This is a larger form of woodwork. Once you attain professionalism and show competence to work on larger projects, you could be contracted to do woodwork. This includes interior and exterior work in the home or yard. Paneling, decorative wood accents, ornate fences are many ways of using the scroll saw at home. To get this type of contract, you just need to properly position yourself for the opportunity. This kind of work can keep you busy for weeks and you are sure to have short breaks where there are no contracts, you can use that period to build your portfolio and improve your skill. You just have to ensure your work is impressive because that is the only way you can get a callback or referral from your client.

6. Teach Scroll Sawing:

   A quote reads thus, "the best way to recreate magic is not by making more magic but by training more magicians." If you ask me, this is the most satisfying task here. Teaching scroll sawing will help you sharpen your expertise and give you the privilege of building more scrollers.

Talk more about when you are now teaching for the money. You can organize a program in your community to teach young persons saw scrolling for a penny. After the training, you have the choice of recruiting them and expanding your workforce to bring you faster and more deals.

Chapter 2

Saw Scrolling Tips and Tricks

Using a scroll saw could be quite technical or tricky. You can't achieve certain types of designs if you don't know how to carefully and smartly use the scroll saw. It is not enough to know how to handle the scroll saw; you would want to make creative wood patterns. To achieve a high level of creativity in your woodworking, you have to know how to use this saw well enough. Compiled in this chapter is a list of tips and tricks that will make you a master in a saw scrolling and make your early years as a saw scroller easy. Let's dive in.

1. Align your blade to be squared with the table.

Positioning is very important and a necessary item of consideration in saw scrolling to achieve the best result and avoid common mistakes people make in saw scrolling. Even if you have a table that tilts the saw arm, ensure that your blade is positioned at a right (90°) angle to the saw table. This is very important to position your blade before sawing, especially when you are stack cutting, cutting puzzles, or compound projects.

2. Sand the wood before cutting.

Sanding your wood before cutting makes it easier to give the wood a perfect facelift and do a good finishing after cutting. The cutting process is usually fuzzy and quite rough; it will do your wood greater good if you do most of your sanding first. Sanding makes it easier and safer for you to work on especially delicate fretwork.

3. Place cut pieces back in place.

After cutting, you still need to sand especially when you're working on portraits. It's okay to leave some of the smaller frets open in the portrait, but you would have to take a different approach when working on larger open spaces. Replace the cut-out wood before you start to sand to protect the fragile bridges. If you sand it without putting the cut-out, you might break the fragile bridges and cause damage to your work.

4. Finish fretwork before assembling.

Before you assemble your work together, ensure that you finish the fretwork. To assemble, mask off the glue joints with tape. Apply the finish to the fretwork, remove the tape, and then glue and clamp the pieces together.

5. Sand after cutting 10 frets

The cutting process is very long especially when you are making portraits. When you are cutting, you tend to produce fuzzies on the bottom of the blank. This is why you should ensure you sand the wood after cutting if not, these fuzzies will lift the blank off the saw table and skew your cuts. You wouldn't want that, so as you cut, take frequent pauses to sand your wood.

6. Take your time cutting thick wood.

Because of the fragility of the saw blade, some persons believe it is not possible to use it in cutting thick wood. This is not true in any way. The blade is not fragile as it appears; the scroll saw has a very firm and strong blade that is easily manipulative. However, you have to be careful when using it on harder and thicker woods. Don't be in a hurry to cut. This will help your blades last longer and stronger. If you happen to push the blank too hard into the blade, it can bend the shape of the blade and skew your cuts.

7. Apply tape to your blank to reduce burning.

Some woods burn very easily, like the black cherry. To prevent the wood from burning, you have to use a lubricant and tape. The lubricant keeps the tape from sticking to itself and greases the blade. This way, it prevents the wood from burning. There are two main ways through which you can achieve this. The first method is by attaching the pattern to the blank with spray adhesive, after which you cover the pattern with clear painter's tape. The other method is by covering the blank with blue painter's tape and then attaching the pattern to the tape.

8. Use clamps and scrap wood to hold compound-cut blanks firmly.

These blanks are slim, and it can be hard to keep them flat on the saw table. Ensure to use quick-grip clamps and flat scrap wood so that the blanks can have more surface area to help them stay flat on the table.

9. Use spray adhesive to attach your pattern to clear shelf paper.

Use a strong adhesive to stick your pattern to the shelf paper. Then, cut out the patterns from the paper. After that, attach them to your blanks. The shelf paper stays firmly, but it can easily remove without leaving a residue.

10. Drill blade-entry holes in small groups.

When you're dealing with intricate portraits with many frets to cut, drill the blank with blade-entry holes in groups of 50. This takes about 45 minutes to cut.

11. Preparing your material and blades carefully before you start saw scrolling.

It is very important that you prepare every other material you will need before you start saw scrolling. It will help you to be more relaxed while you work. Though the scroll saw itself is a very basic component when you want to make a project, you still need to get the other tools ready.

Just like when a chef wants to serve a meal in a restaurant, he won't do that without proper preparation first. In the same vein, you shouldn't begin cutting without preparation.

The better your preparation, the better the quality of your work.

12. Check the blade and blade tension.

During your preparation, ensure to check the blade and measure its tension if it is sufficient for the kind of wood you're working on and the project type you want to do. The effectiveness of the scroll saw is in the ability of the blade.

Also, make sure you're using the correct blade type for the job and that the blades are in good working condition. Trust me, you'll be beyond frustrated using blunt blades or blades with incorrect size – so this is much more important.

There are so many dangers that broken blades can do. They are inexpensive, and it's an inconvenience for you.

You have to look at your blades to make sure they're in good condition. Afterward, it is time to adjust the blade tension.

It takes longer to learn and it is a little tricky.

The tension of the blade can have a direct effect on your wood. When it is too loose, it can cut through anything, and it can fall out of the clamp. If the blades are too tense, you're at the risk of damaging the blades either by breaking or bending.

If you are adjusting the blade, it can be done in several ways. You'll be lucky if you have a scroll saw with a blade adjusting knob/lever. This way you'll be able to use it to find the correct tension.

However, if you want to use a scroll saw that does not have this function, you'll have to rely on your senses to analyze the correct tension. This can be achieved by setting the blade so that it will produce a note, similar to the strings on a guitar. If the sound is too high, it could mean that the blade is too tense. If the sound is too low, it means that the blade is too loose.

For a perfect pitch, endeavor to use guitar tuning devices and apps to monitor the blades' sound. If you do this consistently, you will become accustomed to how these blades sound.

13. Use dry wood.

Another tip that seems a little obvious is that you have to use dry wood. During storage, there is a chance that your wood can become wet. Hence, do a thorough check on your wood before working with it.

Working with wet woods will cause you to miss important points while cutting.

14. Join a woodworking or saw scrolling community.

One way to become a professional in a particular craft is to link up with like minds and professionals in that field. Ensure you participate in club meetings. It will broaden your mind and educate you.

15. Table position and preparation.

Even as you prepare your tools, it is also important that the table is well-positioned. So many scrollers don't know this; thus, they end up making mistakes. Most scroll saws come with an adjustable table. You can bevel left and right to a maximum of 45°.

Position your scroll saw in a particular position before adjusting the bevel. Whether you're sitting or standing, the best position for the scroll saw table is directly in line with your mid-torso.

Also, make sure the blade is in line with your table and not leaning in another direction. The position of your table affects the proficiency of your cut.

Chapter 3

Getting Started with Saw Scrolling

Tools and Supplies

You must use good material in saw scrolling; this will make you more relaxed while you work and make your saw scrolling easy. You'll be able to make your projects faster and easier. Also, it helps you to be coordinated when working.

This is why you must get the right tools and supplies for your woodwork project. It will help you work effectively and efficiently. You will have a perfect outcome at the end of the day.

Wood

The wood type is very necessary to consider as they determine the full impact of the blade on the wood. The best wood type must be hard-wearing but still soft enough that it won't break your saw. A very thin material will give you less control. A harder and dense material will risk the increase in vibration due to the resistance caused by the density of the material. Choosing the wrong wood can lead to the breaking or bluntness of your blade. On the other hand, you could also be at the risk of losing your wood through burning or chipping. Hence, you have to ensure that you select the right wood to get the best result or reproduce the best pattern for your project.

This leads us to the categories of wood we have to check out; Hard or Softwood.

Both types of wood have their demerits and merits. Softer wood is popularly believed to be the best wood for practice. As a beginner, the best wood you can use for practice is the softwood, as it allows you to easily penetrate with the scroll saw and manipulatively use the saw in making cuts. Mastering control over the saw could be one big task, so as a starter, you need to use a wood that will allow you to wield that control fully. However, you have to be careful because softer wood could easily break if the pressure is too much and the frets are too close.

There are several types of softwood; some of them are so soft that they could just break or chip once they are under any form of pressure or duress. There are the much firmer ones still under this category of softwood. Not all softwoods are soft and useless. Some are still firm enough to be used in saw scrolling.

You can use cedar and plywood, but avoid using pine wood. It is very much fragile and could chip during cutting because it has thin grains. The best softwood to use is poplar wood; it has more grains than all the other woods and is more stable. With the poplar wood, you can cut at an even speed without having to worry about changing the tension of the blades to reduce the sharpness of the blade.

The plywood is a good choice also; it has good tensile strength and is very stable, but it could eat through your blades faster than a normal wood would. On the contrary, some woodworkers use this wood because it is relatively cheap and very much affordable. It also has a sharp and very attractive appearance.

For hardwoods, there are so many great woods that you could pick from this category if hardwood is your thing. A long list of hardwood that is used in saw scrolling is the red oak, walnut, cherry, saw sub, hickory, ash, and maple.

Let's start from the last down to the first. The ash and maple wood are mainly considered woods for professionals. They are favored and have this very hard grain that makes it difficult to cut through. They are likely to vibrate, smoke, jump up and down during cutting. It requires a great degree of skill to pull together.

The hickory and saw sub are not too different from the ash wood. The saw sub is said to be much easier to use. It has a unique tendency to absorb stain in irregular ways and has a curly grain that could look beautiful after it is cut. The hickory wood is the cheapest amongst all. It also has the highest weight and strength when compared with other woods.

The cherry and walnut also have very tough grains. They are quite difficult to work with as they require much effort to cut into the wood.

The oakwood is most preferred because it is easier to dive into this wood than any other wood. It has strong grains that would resist blunt blades, but if you are with a well-sharpened blade with good tension, you are sure to enjoy working with this wood.

Scroll Saw

There are several brands of scroll saws, but all of them have the same features and almost look alike. Below is an image of the conventional scroll saw.

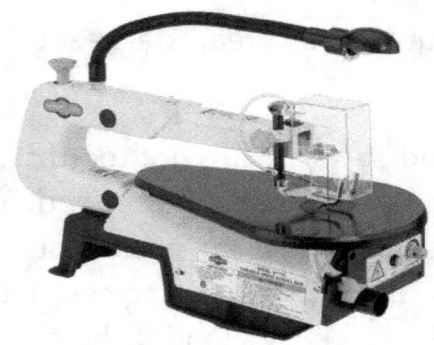

There are many parts of the scroll saw. Before you purchase this saw, you need to know the different parts of the saw and its function. The main parts of the scroll saw include:

- Table: This is the flat surface where you will lie your material for cutting.
- Blade guard: This guard is located very close to the blade. It protects your fingers from sliding into the blade during cutting.
- Blade tension knob: This part of the saw is used in adjusting the tension of the blade. Although it cannot be found in all scroll saws, it is necessary to ensure you are working with the correct blade tension.
- Blade clamps: This is used to lock this blade in place, especially when it is not in use. Most

machines have two clamps. One is located at the top of the table that is connected to the arm, and the other is located at the bottom of the table. You would see a manual on how to use it when you purchase your machine.
- Dust blower: While cutting, sawdust could pile up on your pattern. The dust blower helps you to blow dust from your work surface.
- Throat: This is present in every scroll saw. It is the space between the blade and the back of the scroll saw.
- Tilt lock knob: This is the 90 degrees turner. It helps you adjust the table to do miter cuts and make perfect cuts of unique shapes. You can also use it to cut tiny pieces of wood.

Scroll saw's buyer guide

There are different types of scroll saw; they vary in sizes, prices, and features.

Buying a used scroll saw leaves you with the consequence of having to sharpen the blades now and then. You also have to change your blades every once in a while because they will be quick to get obsolete.

Also, depending on the kind of work you intend to use the blades for, you have to pay close attention to the details of the blade. Professional and experienced scrollers usually choose a new saw based on its performance criteria, not necessarily its appearance. Whether it looks beautiful, strong, firm, or whatever, what is most important and worthy of attention is the blade. Your blades are the main tools used in saw scrolling, so they are the most to be considered.

If you are a fretwork portrait artist, you should be interested in something with a large throat depth that allows for cutting deeper projects and top feeding saws in which the blade can be released from the bottom blade holder to the top of the workpiece.

Traditional artists are more important in saws that provide smooth vibration-free cutting and produce perfectly square cuts to the workpiece.

People use pretty expensive saws because they guarantee accuracy and reduce vibration during work. Though the type of model also affects the frequency and vibration.

When you want to buy a scroll saw, there are things that you should consider.

- Arm type: There are three main types of arms that scroll saws usually have. The three of them have pros and cons. The most common and modern one is the parallel arm. The parallel arm has two arms running from the opposite sides parallel to each other. The blade is usually attached to the ends of the arms. This arm and the other two arms have been fully discussed in chapter one.
- The type of blades it accepts: The blade type is also a very basic thing to be checked. There are two major types of blades; pin-end blades and plain end blades. If you buy a scroll saw that uses the pin-end blades, you can't change the blades to a plain end blade.
- Blade changing feature: This is another feature to look out for. Some scroll saws have quick changing features while others have tolled blade changes. You need to look out for a scroll saw that allows you to change blades easily. Tolled scroll saws will require that you use tools whenever you want to change the blade. The quick-change release scroll saw is the better option to use. It is also necessary that you lookout

for a blade changing feature that supports the two types of blades; the pin end and plain end blades.
- Throat length: The throat length dictates the size of material you can work on. A basic scroll saw has a throat that measures between 16-20 inches. There are smaller scroll saws with smaller throat lengths. The bigger the throat length, the larger the material you can work with on the scroll saw.
- Blade tensioning knob: The positioning of the blade tensioning knob is very important. The position determines how easy it is to access and how possible it is to tighten the knob. The best place to have the knob is at the front, as it is very easy to access and tighten the frequency of the blade. The cheaper scroll saws have it at the back; you must avoid using this type of blade.
- Speed: Scroll saws usually have two types of speed. The first type of speed is the revolutions per minute (RPM). The second type of speed consideration is the adjustable speed. Although some say that the first type of speed doesn't matter, the expert states that it is best to look for scroll saws with RPM of between 400 and 1600.

You must get a scroll saw that has both the RPM and adjustable speed function. The single-speed scroll saws are not a great option.

- Dust blower and collection: The dust blower is used to gather and collect saw dusts from the scroll saw. It acts as a temporary receptor for dusts that are clogging the work surface. This system is usually powered by a large induction motor and used to capture woodwork debris into the ductwork or collection area.
- Task lighting: The scroll saw has a LED designed to illuminate the exact spot on the material. The scroll saws offer flexible tube task lighting.
- Hold-down foot: All scroll saws have a hold-down foot that keeps the material pressed firmly to the table. However, some people don't like this feature because it can block vision when you're cutting. The best option is a saw with a hold-down foot made from strong and thin metal. The bulky one is not so much part of the cutting area.

Scroll Saw Adhesives

Most scroll saw projects require that you draw patterns and adhere them to your base. There are many ways of adhering pattern to base, but it is dependent on the wood type and the pattern. The adhesives you use on softwoods might not work on hardwoods. You would have to use an adhesive that has a relatively adaptive feature.

However, before you even start the process of applying the adhesive, ensure that your wood surface is smooth and even. Also, get rid of any form of sawdust, clean it off with a rag.

Here is a brief list of the type of adhesives you can use on softwoods;

- Painters tape
- Graphite
- Elmer's glue spray
- Carbon transfer paper
- Large labels

There are stronger glues or adhesives that people use. However, you are at the risk of removing your wood fibers. Example of this type of glues is the temporary-bond adhesive spray and the clear packaging tape. They can only be used on hardwoods.

There are several types of temporary – bond spray adhesive. Each of them is categorized into gentler and stronger options. The gentler spray adhesives are Elmers glue spray or glue sticks. The stronger adhesives are 3M Adhesive or Loctite. This spray is preferred by many scrollers because, asides from the sweet fact that it is inexpensive, there are always varieties to choose from. One of the best of these adhesives is the 3M Super 77. It dries super-fast and can easily be corrected when a mistake is discovered. However, if you try pulling it after the glue has dried on the wood surface, the glue might pull out the wood fibers, especially if the wood is too soft. This spray is very strong and most advised to be used on stronger woods or firm work surfaces. To effectively remove it without pulling out the wood fibers or causing damage to your pattern, use a good adhesive remover. There are so many brands of them, and you can get one at a fair price from your local store. Ensure to use it in a well-ventilated area and use a respirator, gloves and google to prevent the spray from choking you.

For lighter wood, you can use more friendly glues like Elmer's glue.

Attaching your pattern to your wood is one of the easiest but most critical parts of saw scrolling because you can't effectively cut if you don't attach your patterns properly and in the right manner. There are several ways by which you can attach patterns to the wood surface. The first method is by sticking it directly.

To stick your pattern directly, here is a long step or procedure you have to follow;

First, you are to hold up your pattern in the air to prevent folding or dribbling when covering the wood surface. Next, spray 1-2 coats of glue on the wood, and allow it for 30 seconds to become tacky. This will give it a strong and lasting bond.

Once you've ascertained its tackiness, smooth the wood surface pattern and leave it to dry. The time it takes to dry depends on the quantity and quality of glue you added, the humidity of the room, and the temperature. On average, it should dry in an hour.

The best adhesive option to use for your wood base is the label printer. It is easier to remove than other adhesive patterns. Also, it is less likely to remove wood fibers from your wood.

Clamps

Although some scroll saws come with clamps to hold the material down while you work., some others don't. So, you would have to buy one for yourself. They are also used to secure wood pieces in place until the glue dries up well.

These clamps are not expensive, depending on the type and model you want. The clamps used in saw scrolling are the same clamps used in woodworking. Though, they are less complex and quite simpler to use.

A shortlist of clamps you can use are;

- G or C clamp: This is one very versatile clamp used by woodworkers and scrollers to hold the wood down to glue up and sawed easily. It has a very wide range of selections for you to choose from. The openings of the jaw of this clamp can range from one to eight inches. The screw section can be used to clamp irregular surfaces because of its swivel head. It is usually screwed into the work table.
- Pipe clamp: This clamp is also called the gluing clamp. It is very easy to use, especially when you are working on flat material. You could also use

this clamp when you are saw scrolling metals. The jaw of the clamp is very adjustable, which makes it easy for you to work on longer projects.

- Spring clamp: This clamp, unlike others, isn't screwed to any surface. Also, it can't be used while sawing because it is relatively small. The spring clamp is mainly used in securing two or more pieces together after they have been glued. It has the shape of a peg and a sizeable jaw to hold your wood pieces together.
- Bench clamp: This is the best option of all. It is very similar to the G or C clamp. As the name implies, you would have to screw it into a work table or bench. It is majorly made to hold things on a bench. The jaw is also adjustable in height and length.

Drill Bits

Saw scrolling could require that you drill out a hole first before working to make the process easier and faster for you. Drill bits are majorly used on wood, metal, and sometimes ceramics. If you need a drill bit for metal saw scrolling, you would have to get heavy-duty and very sturdy alternatives to the conventional drill bits commonly used.

Below is a shortlist of drill bits that can be used in drilling.

- Brad-point bits: It has a spur point and a twisted bit. The tip has the shape of 'W'. This allows the drill to penetrate easily into the wood. The outer point starts cutting the hole before the center point. In the end, you have a clean and smooth hole, no matter the texture of the wood. The sizes usually range from 3mm to 10mm.
- Multipurpose bits: Here is an all-rounder in drilling. It can be used to drill through any material like wood, metal, ceramics, plastic, and others. When working on a hard surface, it might require a harmer to create an immediate and clean hole.
- Spade bits: This is one of the most commonly used drills. It is used to drill large and wide holes in wood. It has a wider diameter of 6 to 38mm, so it can be used for bigger projects. It has an adjustable shank attachment that gives it a better grip on the material.

Choosing the Right Scroll Saw Blade

The scroll saw blade determines the efficiency of the scroll saw to a very large extent.

Here is a guide to choosing scroll saw blades:

- Use large blades for thick wood. Use #5 or #7 blade for a medium hardwood around ¾" to 1" thickness. This way, your blades are more liable to breaking, even when you add pressure. They also cut faster and quicker.
- Use small blades for thin wood: These blades will help you to control the blade as you cut. Smaller blades cut slower and are easier to control. This makes them most fitting for thin wood as you won't want to make a sharp mistake in a project when cutting. When cutting frets in a puzzle, this is the best type of blade to use.
- When choosing a blade, consider the blades that will cut tight corners of the wood: In almost all cases, large blades can't cut intricate frets the way small blades would.
- Every blade has a lifetime, so ensure to get blades that have a solid density and thickness: The denser the blade is, the longer it tends to last.

Below is a long list of different scroll saw blades you can select from.

There are two categories of scroll saw blades; plain end blade and pin-end blade. It is best to use a saw that uses both blade types, so you won't get stranded when you run out of a particular blade type.

The pin-end blade can't make deep interior cuts like the plain end-blade. In other words, the plain-end blade is used to make intricate cuts, and the pin-end blade is used to make exterior cuts.

Here is a brief list of blade styles you should look out for.

- Standard tooth blade: This type of blade has its teeth place at an even distance apart. Each blade is separated by the same distance. This blade is nosier than other styles of blades.
- Skip tooth blade: This is a great choice for beginners as they make cutting a little slower. This enables you to manipulate the saw and make unique kinds of cuts without destroying your wood. In the skip tooth blades, there are just a few teeth, the rest are missing.

- Double tooth blade: This is a toothed blade with a wide gap between the only two sets of teeth present in the blade. They will give you a smoother cut than other blades because the blade has just two teeth.
- Reverse tooth blade: This blade prevents tear-out when cutting. It is just like the skip tooth blades. The last few teeth face upwards on the bottom.
- Precision ground tooth blade: These blades are a great choice for cutting straight lines. However, it is very easy to make mistakes with this blade as a beginner. You need to have a strong wield of control over the blade to prevent it from cutting outside your pattern. This blade has a smaller set of teeth. The teeth are mostly wild and ground down instead of being filed.
- Spiral blades: The spiral blades have teeth on all sides. The blades allow you to cut in whatever direction you want. It allows you to express your creativity freely when cutting. However, they don't cut as clean as other blades and can be quite difficult to use. Ensure the blade is used for cutting unique cuts. It is mainly for professionals.

- Crown tooth blades: This tooth is the newest type of blade in saw scrolling. Every second tooth will be pointed in the opposite direction. This blade style is great for cutting plastic.

Scroll Saw Safety Guidelines
- Safety glasses are to be worn at all times. This is to prevent particles from the wood or sawdust from entering the eyes.
- Cover your long hair in a net while working to prevent the machine from trapping the wood.
- Do not wear a lot of jewelry while you work; it could endanger you. Use only simple jewelry.
- Wear sturdy and firm footwear while working to prevent your feet from getting hurt.
- Avoid loose or bogus clothing, it could get trapped in the machine and affect your work progress.
- Some operations might require that you use hearing protection. The machine could get loud and noisy when you are working on a big wood.
- Ensure that the scroll saw is safely kept on a stable surface where it won't fall off or be affected by any other substance.

- Ensure that the workspaces and operation zone is clear of slips, hazards, and trip.
- The scroll saw should be operated on an RCD-protected circuit.
- Place the blade guard in a secured and fixed position.
- Whether in use or not, ensure that the blade teeth are always pointing downwards.
- Immediately you notice a fault in your scroll saw, ensure that you report it already.
- Properly adjust the blade tension at all the time
- Select the correct size and blade type for cutting your woods.
- Before you start to use the saw, start the machine and watch the saw run for a while. If you hear any unfamiliar noise, stop working immediately. Turn the saw off and don't use it until you correct the problem.
- Keep your fingers and hands safely distant from the point of operation of the scroll saw.
- Ensure to use the scroll saw on only firm surfaces like wood, plastics, and nonferrous metals.
- Ensure to switch off the saw immediately after use and reset all guards to a fully closed position.

- Keep a thrown piece by the side to use as a guide in case the blade should break. Also, position your face and body to a side of the blade to prevent the particles from harming you.
- Don't work when you are stressed or unfocused. Your brain needs to be focused on the task when working to help you avoid risks. You are in great danger when you are working without focus.
- Ensure that the work area is well lighted to guide you while you work.
- Keep the ventilation channels open to prevent suffocation from heat and sawdust.
- Ensure your machine is placed securely and firmly on your tabletop or workbench to prevent it from falling off.
- Never turn the saw on before clearing out the table.
- Don't try reaching under the table while the saw is running.

Scroll Saw Essentials
- Squaring the table: Scroll saws usually have an adjustable table that allows you to make simple cuts at various angles. The cutting is done with

the blade placed perpendicularly to the table, and the table is slightly off square. The commonest method of saw scrolling is to use a small metal square or right-angle tool. The process involves setting the square on the saw table beside a blade that has been inserted and tensioned. To make a square cut, saw through a piece of scrap wood and use a square to check the angle of the cut. Keep adjusting the table until you achieve a perfectly cut square.

- Attaching patterns: There are so many sprays and adhesives used in saw scrolling. Out of them all, temporary –bond spray is the most commonly used adhesive. Before you apply the spray to attach the pattern, cover the wood with blue painters' tape to lubricate the wood. This act makes it easier for the pattern to be removed. Apply spray to the back of the paper pattern and glue it to the shelf paper. Cut the pieces out and apply them to the banks. To make a transferred pattern directly to the wood, you can use graphite paper or carbon paper. Carbon paper is more affordable.

- Stack cutting: This is the cutting of many pieces of a project at one time. To achieve this, attach the blanks with tape, align all the layers, wrap a layer up around the outside edge. Asides from wanting to cut the pieces of a project at once, wrapping stacks help the wood to stay stable while you cut. You can use tape or hot melt glue for stacking. Glue the sides of the blanks together.
- Blade entry holes: The best way to cut a pattern out is by marking areas for blade entry holes. If there are no marks for blade entry holes, place the holes near a cut line. The holes shouldn't be placed on a curving line. Drill the hole perpendicular to the blank using a drill press. While drilling, ensure that the holes are vertical. Drill the blank through a scrap piece to prevent it from tearing out at the back and affecting the work surface. For thin cuts, use the smallest drill.
- Blade tension: Before you start working with the machine or insert the blade, remove the tension of the blade. Clamp the two ends of the blade into the blade holders to adjust the tension after you have inserted the blade. A blade that doesn't have enough tension is almost useless because all it

will do is wander from one point to another. A blade that has too much tension would break in no time. The best you can do for the safety of your blade is to set the tension accurately using an external tension marker or guitar tuner if your blade doesn't have one.

How to Finish Scroll Saw Projects

Finishing your scroll saw project is as important as the start because what is the point in doing the project if it is not to make it beautiful.

To make a great saw scrolling project, you need to get the right finish for your project and give it that outstanding look. There are a variety of finishes for you to use on your project. Finishing comes in two ways. After transferring the pattern to your wood and making the cuts, the very next thing is the finishing.

The very first process in finishing is sanding. This will make the edges and surface more attractive. There are many sanders that you can use in the finishing process. You can use the belt sanders and other common sanders used in woodworking. When choosing sanders and sandpapers, you must consider the grit number. There is 120 to 150 or 220 grit paper. The number of grit paper determines the effect it will have on the wood. The higher the number of grit paper, the more intense the effect on the wood. For small pieces, you are to use lower grit paper.

After sanding, the next step is painting. You might want to coat your wood in a new color of paint to give it a whole new look. Painting or coating isn't just necessary for decorative purposes, it is also important that you amplify the beauty of your craft with bright natural colors. You don't need to make it too bright. When choosing paints or coats, you are to consider the odor, thickness of the paint.

Be careful not to choose a paint that has a discomforting odor. This is one thing you should watch out for if you are allergic to smell. Also, the thickness of the paint determines how easy it will be to correct errors, clean up, and how easily or quickly it dries.

The thickness also determines how long it be will last and how well it blocks the UV rays. The UV rays break down the finish so that it cracks, and it can no longer flex. A greater problem comes up when the UV breaks, the finish cracks up, and the wood becomes susceptible to moisture. This whole issue speeds up deterioration.

The best choice for outdoor projects is a properly primed exterior oil plant.

Also, when you are building something outdoor, you have to be careful to choose something that won't wash; the paint or oil you must use should be lasting.

A Short message from the Author:

Hey, I hope you are enjoying the book? I would love to hear your thoughts!

Many readers do not know how hard reviews are to come by and how much they help an author.

I would be incredibly grateful if you could take just 60 seconds to write a short review on Amazon, even if it is a few sentences!

>> Click here to leave a quick review

Thanks for the time taken to share your thoughts!

Chapter 4

Saw Scrolling Projects

There are several designs you can make with the scroll saw. Check them out below

Personalized Tree Plaque

This is a very creative project that anyone can make. It doesn't cost so much to make. It looks uniquely ancient.

Supplies

- Pinewood
- Pencil
- Drill
- Scroll saw
- Hanger hook

Procedures

Step 1: Make a printout of the image on a transparent paper to transfer it to the wood.

Step 2: Trace the design on the wood.

Step 3: Since the leaves and ridges of the trunk need to be cut out, drill tiny holes so the blade can cut through.

Step 4: Start cutting through all the holes till you effectively cut out all the leaves and trunk.

Step 5: Add a wall hanger hook to the back of the plaque. Attach this hook to the plaque and hang it on the wall, or you could just place it on a shelf.

Botanical Trivets

The botanical trivet is a very creative project that allows you to cut some different shapes of leaves. It looks very real, just like a big leaf used as a trivet.

Supplies

- Bamboo or wooden cutting boards
- Botanical printables
- Scissors
- 120 grit sandpaper
- Scroll saw
- Bright colors
- Bowl finish

Procedures

Step 1: Search the internet and print the type of botanical leaf of your choice on a piece of paper.

Step 2: Trace and cut out the shape with scissors.

Step 2: Layout the paper stencil on your cutting board and trace it out with a pen or pencil.

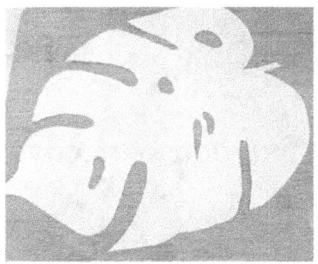 

Step 4: After tracing it out, your wood is ready for cutting. Use the scroll saw to make a perfect cut on your wood.

Step 5: Sand your wood until it appears bare and porous

Step 6: They are cool the way they are but for a great effect, you would have to apply a color of your choice.

Step 7: Use a finish that coats the wood perfectly. Your trivet is ready.

Wooden Utensil Trivet

This design looks very interesting, like a burst of utensils. Like the botanical trivet, this is also used as a mat to place cups, plates, and pots. However, it is bigger and more multipurpose. You can use this trivet both indoors and outdoors.

But it is majorly an indoor eating material. It's a utensil trivet, so it's an eating thing. Or what do you think?

Supplies

- 12 ×12 slab of wood
- Scroll saw
- Utensil design cut from vinyl

Surprised the supplies are very few? Well, that's one very interesting thing about this project. It is easy to make and very natural. You don't need to do so much; let's just get into it.

Procedures

Step 1: Create a combination of utensils on vinyl. If you don't have the time for this, you can purchase it from a shop.

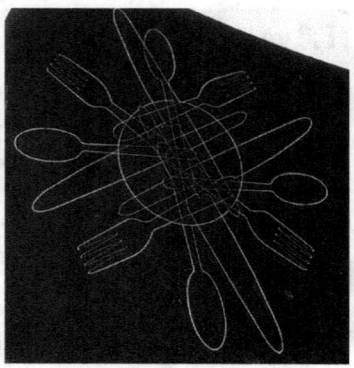

Step 2: Place it down on a transfer paper. Press it until the whole shape is transferred to the paper.

Step 3: Place this paper on the wood to transfer the image. Press it in to ensure that it sits well on the middle of the slab.

Step 4: Leave the vinyl on the wood and carefully cut out the shape of the utensil trivet with your scroll saw.

Rainbow Planter Sconce

Rainbow is such a happy sight. You might want to have this decorative art at a corner of your house to help you light the atmosphere with joy and happiness.

Supplies

- 1*10 board, cut to any size you want
- A large bowl for tracing template
- A scroll saw
- Terra cotta pot
- Cup for tracing template
- Drill
- Miter saw
- Paint or marker

Procedures

Step 1: Get your wood and lay it flat on your working table, facing the surface you want to use upwards.

Step 2: Afterward, place your bowl on the wood, and make an arc using a pencil.

Step 3: Slice around that curve with a scroll saw.

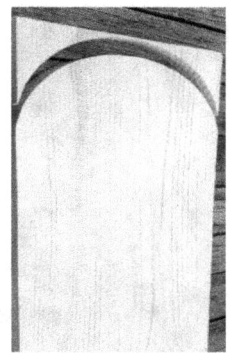

Step 4: Draw the same rounded curve on the other edge of the wood.

Step 5: Use your terra cotta pot to create a round circular shape 1 inch from the rounded edge.

Step 6: Cut the wood in two at about 1 inch from the side of the small circle, using your miter saw.

Step 7: Drill a hole, so you can feed your scroll saw blade into the hole.

Step 8: Cut out the circle and the outer edges.

Step 9: It is time to throw in the colors. Feel free to add as many colors as you want, but also watch out for the alignment. Make sure there is a line guiding your coloring so you don't color roughly. It is best to use a color marker. Also, endeavor to leave some space in the middle so the little plant in the pot won't cover the rainbow design as it grows.

Step 10: Place a cup in the hole of the cutout wood. That will serve as a vase for the flower, and the wood will be a little shelf.

Step 11: Affix the half-cut to the rainbow backboard. You must have made a mark to highlight where you wanted your shelf to be. Drill a hole at the two ends of the wood for screwing. Glue the little shelf before screwing it in for firmer support.

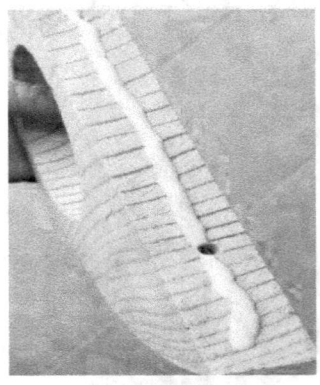

Step 12: Place the flower in the vase or cup, and your rainbow planter is ready. You can make several more.

Wood and Macrame Plant Wall Hanger

Thinking of a creative piece to give your house a facelift? This wall hanger is just perfect!

Supplies

- Pine board
- Scroll saw
- Wood glue
- Macramé cord
- Eye hook
- Wooden ring for macramé
- Painter or color
- Pin nailer

Procedures

Step 1: Decide the length you want your planter to be, and cut out two lengths of that measurement from your board. Draw a horizontal line at the center with the center.

Step 2: Draw the shape of the wall hanger that you want on the wood. This particular tutorial drew an arc to a teardrop-shaped planter. You can choose the same because this tutorial is based on the tear-shaped planter.

Step 3: Cut out the arc using the scroll saw, and use it to mark and cut out others for even measurement. You would be needing about four arcs.

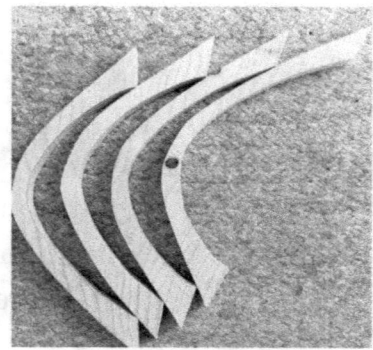

Step 4: Use the scrap woods that are left over from cutting the bows to cut the length of the little notches that will be used to secure the top and bottom of all four pieces together.

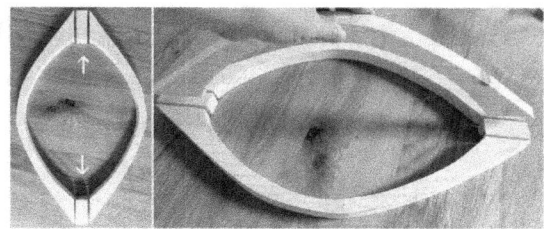

Step 5: The assembly step is quite simple. Start gluing the pieces together, and use the pin nailer to hold it firmly. A clamp would have been a great option, but it wouldn't be possible because of the shape of the arc

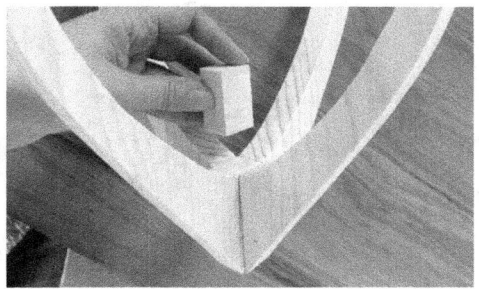

Step 6: Now, you have fixed the top and bottom of the arc. You can begin painting now. Choose your preferred paint and allow it to dry after painting.

Step 6: Use a simple macramé rope to hang the ark. To insert the rope into the ark, screw in an eye hook on top of the planter. Place the vase on the arc.

Scrolly Scalloped Mirror

If you ask me, the scrolly scalloped mirror project is very unique. Know that feeling when you see something in a local store and have this great conviction that you can do it, and then voila! It looks like you transited wood into a miracle piece. The truth is, you don't know what you can do until you give it a try.

Here is a little supply you need to get this done. One interesting thing about this project is that you don't need so much to get it done.

Supplies

- A mirror
- A piece of wood
- A photo design

Procedures

Step 1: Get a photo design (note that this design is going to be used to form the shape of your mirror eventually.) transfer this image to a slab of MDF by first printing it on transparency

Step 2: Cut the entire outside of the design with a scroll saw. Afterward, drill holes on the inside parts that need to be cut. This hole will help you insert the scroll saw for a faster and more effective cutting. After cutting out the edges, endeavor to sand them.

Step 3: Use your preferred paint color and paint the piece.

Step 4: Affix a mounting tape to the body of the project and attach the mirror to it. The mounting tape is very firm. You don't need any other thing.

Step 5: Attach the wood to the design and glue.

Circle Monogram Pallet Wood Décor

This is such a simple project and basic for someone who is just starting to practice saw scrolling. You should try this out; it will help you perfect your scrolling skills.

Supplies

- Pinewood
- Outdoor wood glue
- Biscuit jointer and biscuits
- Pipe clamps
- Paint
- Circle cutting jig
- Scroll saw

Procedures

Step 1: Assemble the pinewood and make a messy stripe of colors on the wood. Leave to dry.

Step 2: Once it gets dry use medium sandpaper to sand it real hard to have the below effect.

Step 3: Add terra cotta to give it a polished look.

Step 4: Join the wood together using biscuit jointer and wood glue to keep it together as one board

Step 6: Wipe off excess glue and leave it clamped overnight. To draw the circle, turn over the board, lay it flat on your work table and drill a 1/8 inch pilot hole at the center. Place the circle cutting jig threaded spur into the hole.

Step 7: Measure and set the location of the circle jig as you want. The location will determine the size of the circle.

Step 8: Set the depth of your plunge router to 1/8 – ¼ inch. Start the router and rotate the circle jig in a counter-clockwise motion. Keep going round and round until the circle is cut out.

Step 9: Print or write the letter K at the center of the circle.

Step 10: Use the scroll saw to cut out the letter K. You would achieve something like this. Awesome!

Butterfly Silhouette Clock

This is an ancient art piece revived presently and more pronounced. It is a very beautiful decorative piece.

You might have to check out this clock in a local store; you'll be surprised at how expensive it is. However, you can make it yourself at a far cheaper price and with little stress.

Supplies

- Printed copies of butterfly
- 24" slab of plywood
- A bowl to make the shape of a round clock
- Clock kit
- Comb hook

Procedures

Step 1: Print three different sizes of butterflies on paper and cut them out.

Step 2: Get your wood and place your bowl over it. Use your pen to draw a circle using the bowl.

Step 3: Trace the butterfly on the wood.

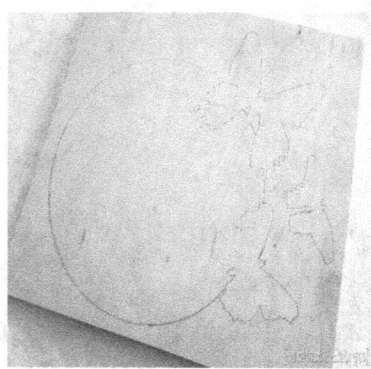

Step 4: Use the scroll saw to cut out the shapes you have drawn. First, cut out the butterflies before cutting out the circle. Take your time when cutting, do not be in a hurry.

Paint the wood with bright colors as you desire, then drill a hole in the middle of the clock. Make sure it is the same size as the clock shaft you purchased.

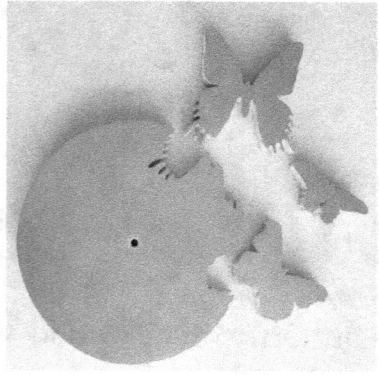

Step 5: Make space for inserting the back of the clock on the wood, and add the clock hands on the clock following the instruction on the package. Put the comb hook on the back of the clock so you can easily hang the clock.

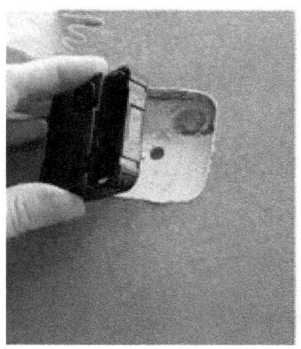

You can use whatever fly you want to use. This project is easy to do and very relatable.

Bracket-Shaped Barn Board Sign

This board sign makes a perfect gift to a family or friend. You could customize the name of a loved one on this board.

Supplies

- 1*4 or 1*6 pine boards
- Stain
- Leftover latex paint in any color
- White acrylic paint
- Chalk marker
- Scroll saw
- Sealer
- Wall hooks

Procedures

Step 1: Print out any bracket shape on flat paper. Project the image on paper using an overhead projector. Ensure that the image is no longer than your board. Trace the shape of the bracket from the paper and cut it out.

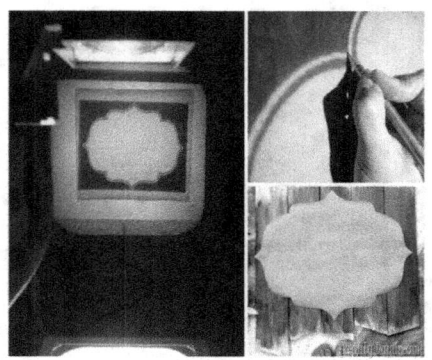

Step 2: Place this pattern on the center of your board and trace it again. Use your pencil or marker to trace it on the wood again. Cut the shape out with a scroll saw.

Step 3: Now, you have that beautiful piece staring at you.

Step 4: Select your preferred font and print it on transparency. Project it through a projector and trace the sign on the wood using a white colored pencil.

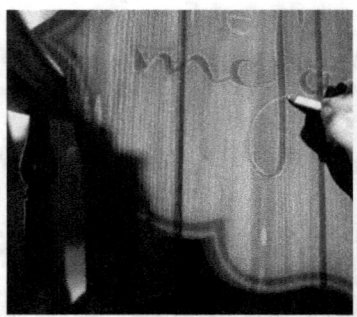

Step 5: Ensure your hands are steady as you paint and use a water-based sealer to prevent it from washing away. You could also decide to paint the edges, it is all up to you. This is incredibly beautiful.

State/ Country Plaque

This is a unique way of making a map. Ever thought of making your plaque of state or country map instead of getting a customized one in the market. What's the point when you can make one yourself.

Supplies

- A thick wood
- The printed image of your state or country map.
- Scroll saw

Procedures

Step 1: Transfer your state map image to the wood through a projector and transparency, like in step 1 above.

Step 2: Carefully trace it out on the paper using a very thick pencil or marker. This will help you to make accurate and careful cuts.

Step 3: Use the scroll saw to make your cuts.

Step 4: Apply color stain to coat the wood and give it a bright finish.

Step 5: You can also add a sticker at any location of your choice, and a wall hook to hang this on the wall.

Mother's Day Plaque

This is a very interesting project and it involves very simple processes you would want to try. It is very similar to the name puzzle. If you are good with the name puzzle, you will not have a problem carrying out this project. This particular idea was born by someone; you can make your creative word puzzle.

Supplies

- 8.5" * 11" board
- A projector and transparency
- A red felt

Procedures

Step 1: Print your artwork on transparency and project it into the wood like in step 1 above

Step 2: Trace the letters "MOTHER" in your artwork. Drill a hole on each of the 'MOTHER' letters. Use the scroll saw to cut out each of the letters.

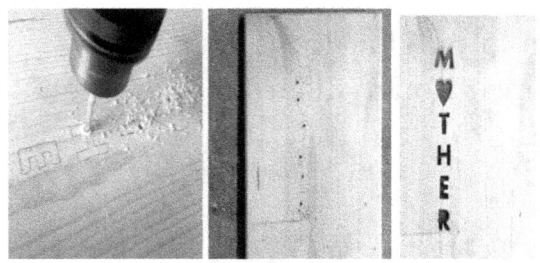

Step 3: Spray a light coat of white spray paint and let it dry for an hour. Sand the wood with 80 grit sandpaper till you can see the woodgrain. Also, apply a little stain on the wood to give it a coated look.

Step 4: Trace the rest of the letters to be bold, and paint them with white paint.

Step 5: Staple or glue the red felt to the back of the wood to come through the front of the wood.

Step 6: Drill two holes by the corner and attach the eye hooks. String a ribbon through the eye hooks and hang it on the wall

.

Custom Corbels

This design is very common in woodworking and furniture. It is majorly used in the making of breakfast bar and table. There are so many designs of the corbel, that you can experiment with when making corbel. This corbel is used in wood crafts, and it is used in designing the house. For each of these purposes, there are different sizes of corbels you can use.

Supplies

- Hard Wood
- Transparency and photocopying machine
- Pencil
- Scroll saw

Procedures

Step 1: You can take a photograph of this corbel design and transfer it to an angle so you can replicate it.

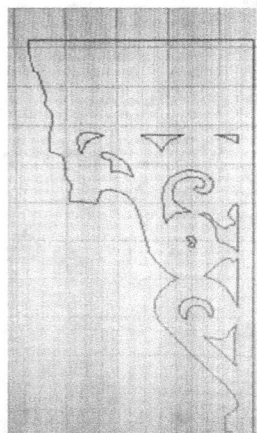

Step 2: Trace the design on the paper using a sharpie so the lines would be very bold, and project it on a piece of paper.

Step 3: You only need to design one side because you are making two detailed sides of the corbel.

Step 4: Cut out this design from the paper using an Exacto knife. Trace the template on the wood and use the scroll saw to make the cut-out.

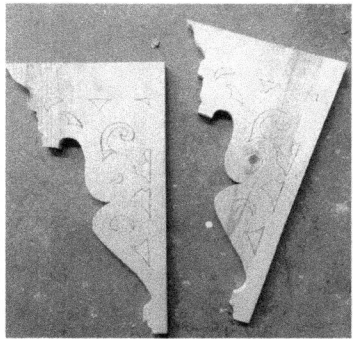

Step 5: Carefully drill holes into the corbel so you can cut them out in the right places individually.

Step 6: Carve the center layer. Make a simple design on it, coat it in dark stains using a cloth, and an old craft brush to paint the nooks and crannies.

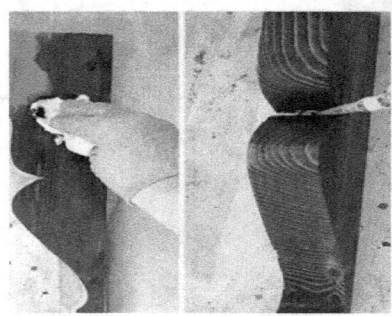

Step 7: Spray the two main sides of the corbel white, and glue all three of them with glue. Use a clamp to hold them firmly for a few minutes to ensure it is well dried.

Step 8: Drill a hole for screwing the corbel to another surface.

Fall-Themed Monogram Wreaths

The beauty of these wreaths is that they can be displayed indoors and outdoors too. They have this unique beauty about them that you can't seem to get enough of. It is not so easy to make, but expect to have massive fun working on this project.

Supplies

- ½" plywood
- Scroll saw
- Paint
- Vanish

Procedures

Step 1: First of all, create a monogram customized to suit your need. Feel free to experiment with really cool monogram fonts.

Step 2: Also, select a round or spherical design with an opening in the middle. For an example of designs, you can select apple, pumpkin, pawpaw, spiderweb, etc.

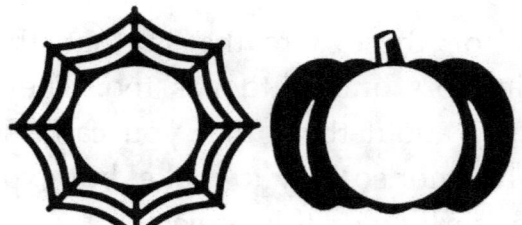

Step 3: Project your image onto your board using an overhead projector and trace the design with a pencil.

Step 4: Trace the initials from the monogram into the board too and allow them to overlap.

Put a mark on the areas that would need to be cut out. In this tutorial, the mark placed was the letter X.

Step 5: Drill holes in all the areas you would be cutting out, as you can see in this image.

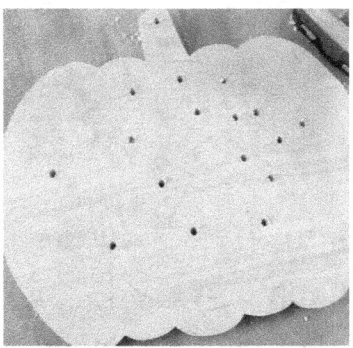

Step 7: Start to scroll out each section carefully till you have something like this.

Step 8: Apply any color of your choice and dab at it using a white cotton cloth. A flower would make this look incredibly gorgeous.

Wooden Paper Doll

Keeping the attention of a child is one big duty today. Children have a short attention span, so you have to get something unique and very creative to capture their attention for a long time.

This wooden paper doll is one of its kind. It is easy to do and a very smart project.

Supplies

- Scrap wood or wooden tray
- Printout of paper doll
- White paint
- 20 grit sandpaper
- Hardwood
- White frets

Procedures

Step 1: Spray your wooden tray in white

Step 2: Browse for a paper doll that has the features you want. Print it on cardstock and carefully cut it out with scissors.

Step 3: Press the paper doll into the wood while it is still wet. This way, it won't need glue to stick in, it will automatically settle well into the wood and lightly sand the wood with a 220-grit sandpaper

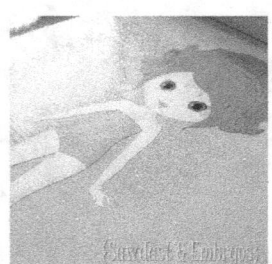

Step 4: Print another doll and use it as a template to trace many doll's clothing on a hardwood.

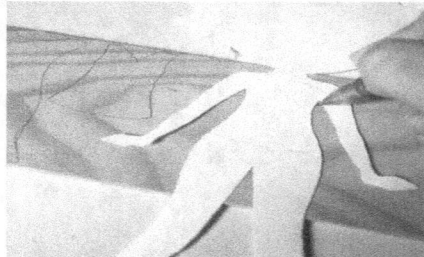

Step 5: Use the scroll saw to cut out the clothing from the hardwood. Sand your clothing items and prime.

Step 6: Feel free to have fun with various colors. Use different coats to color the clothing. Once your painting is dry, use markers and pencils to make other simple designs.

Step 7: Also, add small pieces of clothing to the doll on the tray.

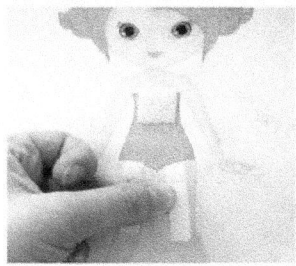

Step 8: Use lines of white frets to decorate the two sides of the plywood, glue the clothing to the two sides of this felt.

Your wooden paper doll is very much ready.

Cutout Silhouette Plaques

This is a very creative project that involves not just hard skills but soft skills. It requires the use of software to create patterns representing children's heads. This plaque is used in place of picture frames. They are also used for identification.

Supplies

- Photographs of children or a child
- Photo editing software
- Printer paper
- Scrap wood
- Scroll saw

Procedures

Step 1: Position the children in such an awkward position where they are staring into an angular distance and take them a photograph. You should be able to achieve something like this.

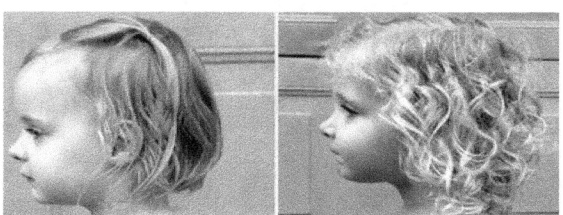

Step 2: Use photo editing software to trace out the curve of their head. Transfer to another document and print a well-detailed shape of the head of the children.

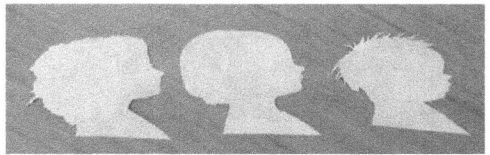

Step 3: Trace this printed head on the scrap rectangular wood using a pencil. If your wood needs to be adjusted in shape, feel free to do that with a bandsaw.

Step 4: Use the scroll saw to carve out the design from the wood.

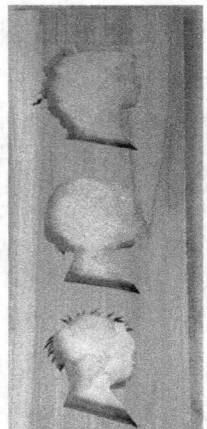

Step 5: Sand the edges to be round and decorative.

Step 6: Get a fresh slab of wood to be used as a frame for the plaque. Spray it in thick black

Step 7: Join the plaque and the frame or backboard using glue.

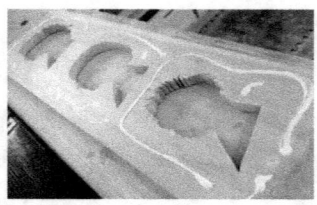

Step 8: Put a comb hook at the back of this great piece so it can be placed where everyone can see and admire it.

Wooden Typography Artwork

Some websites allow you to see the typography of your location. You will need a lot of wood for this project to highlight the flow of the typography. There are so many layers of land you would need to represent, and the only means of representation is the wood. This project can be used to teach geography.

Supplies

- A stack of 1/8" wood.
- Print out of land typography

Procedures

Step 1: Print out the typography of your chosen location and number all the layers in your typography. Cut every number out as you trace it.

Step 2: Bring a new board for each new layer and keep coming till the tiniest lump.

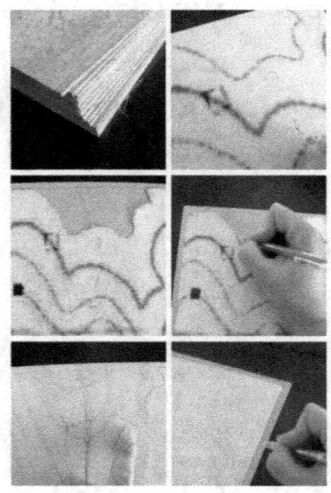

Step 3: Cut out the borders or frames from all the woods, and learn the demand. Use the scroll saw to cut out the design and shape of the maps.

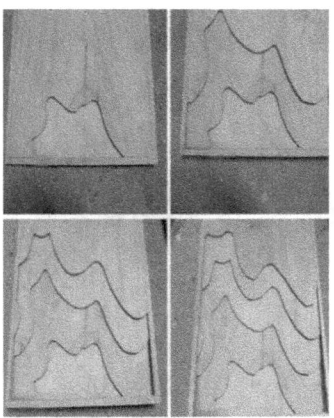

Step 4: Assemble them like you can see in the photo and attach a border.

Step 5: You are to glue them together. Use a small brush to glue on these narrow edges. Use acrylic paint to stain the wood layers.

You can place a hook behind it. Your typography frame is ready.

Wooden Arrow Name Plaques

This is another name design. It is very innovative and creative. You can customize the names of your children on this plaque.

Supplies

- Slab of hardwood
- Chalk marker
- Drill
- Scroll saw
- Wood glue

- Paint
- Sandpaper
- Picture hanger
- Plywood for substrate
- 1*10 pine board

Procedures

Step 1: Print the name "Mollie" on a transparency. The name is printed in script font.

Step 2: Use cardstock to draw out the edges of the name and the sketch of the arrow.

Step 3: Project the image to your wood and trace it boldly.

Step 4: Sketch a rough diagram of an arrow to make it look like a sharpie, just like you have in the image above.

Step 5: Cut off the bulk of the edges with a band saw, so the wood has a very stable shape.

Also, drill holes in all the letters to enable you to be able to cut it with a scroll saw

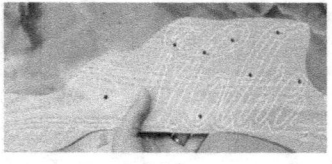

Step 6: Cut the name out with a scroll saw, and sand the cut-out letters with a 220 sandpaper

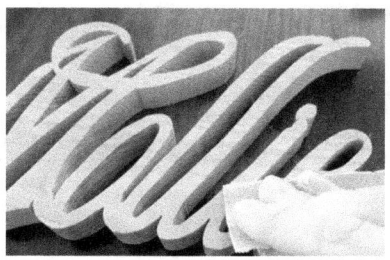

Step 7: Glue this to the pine board

Step 8: Paint your wood your desired color and add a substrate to the back of the pine board so you can easily hang the board.

Step 9: Attach hangers to the back of the wood and let it be.

Wooden Logo Sign

This is a unique project you could try. Instead of hiring the services of a designer to design you a logo banner to place in front of your mall or shop, you could make this simple logo sign with just the following supplies.

Supplies

- Pinewood big enough for the size you want to make your logo
- ½" plywood for backer board
- 220 grit sandpaper
- Vinyl decal
- Adhesives
- Scroll saw

Procedures

Step 1: Get a vinyl decal of the design you want to use for your logo

Step 2: Glue this design to your pinewood and use the scroll saw to cut the logo out.

Step 3: You could get a vinyl decal of the letters also and glue it to the wood. Carefully use your scroll saw to cut out these letters.

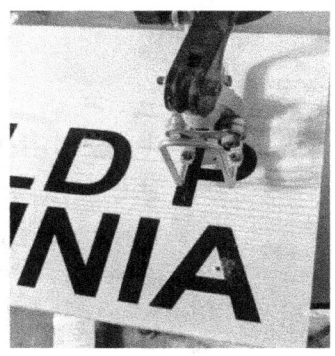

Step 4: Assemble the logo and letters on fresh hardwood to check out how they look. You should be having something of this fashion. Cute right?

Step 5: Cut your backer board or plywood to your desired size and sand it with your sandpaper for a little while before applying the coat of black paint.

Step 6: Build a simple frame using a router and nail gun.

Step 7: Allow the paint for about thirty minutes to dry. After which, you assemble the logo and letters on the board using a ruler to align them together.

Step 8: Glue it all in place, and your wood logo is ready. You can add a hook on the back of the board for hanging the piece.

Name Puzzle

Looking for a fun project to keep the kids busy during summer? Here is one special one for you. It is not decorative, but it is very easy and simple to make. You would have to use a unique font in making this puzzle, unlike the normal children puzzle you see around.

Supplies

- ½" plywood
- Pencil and sharpie for tracing
- Drill
- Scroll saw

Procedures

Step 1: Use a unique font to write the name you want to use on your computer, then project it to your wood.

Step 2: Use the pencil and sharpie to trace it boldly

Step 3: Drill holes on the letters to enable you to insert the scroll saw and cut through the letters

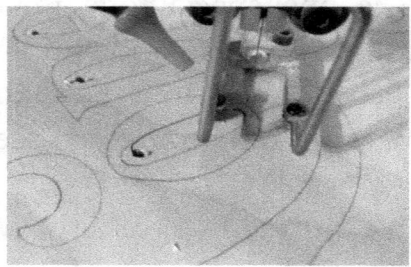

Step 4: Carefully cut the insides of the letters using the scroll saw. Scroll out the delicate parts first to prevent error.

Step 5: After cutting the insides of the letter, cut the whole letter out.

Step 6: Sand the letters carefully to get the fuzziness off. Use an orbital sander to sand the flat surface of the puzzle board.

Step 7: Place the puzzle board upon another wood with ¼" thickness, and trace out the letters through the puzzle board on the backer board with your sharpie.

Step 8: Glue the two boards together and paint the openings of the puzzle.

Step 9: Use a clamp of heavy objects to press the wood together to be well glued together.

Step 10: Put the traced letters inside a black coat and allow them to dry.

Step 11: Insert the letters into the puzzle board.

Personalized Picture Plaque

This is a unique picture plaque; the idea is just so unusual. This photo plaque has a peg. You won't find this plaque in any store. This is the beautiful thing about saw scrolling; it allows you to make things out of your imagination. You have borne innovative ideas out of your head.

Supplies

- 20"*6" slab of plywood
- Alphabet stencils
- Drill
- Scroll saw
- Tiny clothespins
- Glue
- Hook for wall hanger

Procedures

Step 1: Arrange your alphabet stencil on the slab of plywood and trace the alphabet stencil on the wood.

Step 2: Drill a hole through the wood, and insert the saw to cut through the wood.

Step 3: Carefully cut out the letters from the slab of plywood, mark and sand the edges to make it round.

Step 4: Glue the clothespins to the wood and arrange them like the one in the picture. Place the pins parallel to the letters on the plaque.

Step 5: Attach the hook to the back of the plaque and hang it at the spot. You could use the pins to hang your pictures.

Chapter 5

Fixing Common Saw Scrolling Problems

You may encounter some problems as you use your scroll saw. Now, not to worry because, in this chapter, I have curated a list of the possible challenges and ways to remedy these problems.

Common Problems with Saw Scrolling

Heat-related problems

Like most machines, intense heating generally reduces the efficiency of work and can result in loss of work. Hence, if you experience heating problems with your scroll saw device, what could be the cause? If your machine is overworked, then overheating is very much possible. Other factors which contribute to the heating problem include the wrong choice of blade, blunt blades, and working with heavy/thick materials.

To remedy this, you should always use the right blade on the right wood. A wrong choice of the blade on wood will make your scroll saw device overheat. Here is the simple configuration: the big blades are designed for thick wooden plaques and smaller blades for less dense plaques.

Once you notice an overheating, all you need to do is unplug your device from the socket and let it cool off for a while. If the problem persists after you've done all of this, then you have to contact the manufacturer. However, I'm convinced that using the right and sharp blades on the right wood should give you the best effect.

Exploded fuses and tripped breakers

Fuses are components that regulate the rate at which the current flows into a circuit. Like most machines powered by electricity, scroll saws require a lot of electric power that can even blow up fuses and trip breakers.

In case your scroll saw device ceases to function suddenly, you should check your fuse box immediately. This is because, in this case, the problem has little or nothing to do with the tool's functionality. You should note that when firing your scroll saw back up after tripping a breaker or blowing up a fuse, set it at the lowest blade speed initially. Then, you can begin to work your blade speed up from there.

Table Vibrations

The advantage of the scroll saw's removable blade is that it allows you to make interior cuttings without the need for an entry slot. However, the downside is that its reciprocating cutting action can cause the work table to vibrate aggressively. Hence, it can become challenging to make detailed cuts relevant to your work. If the portion of the table of your scroll saw vibrates up to the extent you can press down to keep the work piece in place, then you must find a solution.

To solve this, you must first place your scroll saw on a clean and flat surface. The reason is you'll much likely have issues with table vibrations if the saw's base is not entirely flush with the surface. Then, if your c-clamps are unavailable, secure the saw to the work surface it is placed upon. This would help reduce the table vibrations to a great extent. The final thing to do if table vibrations persist completely inhibit productivity, then consider upgrading your scroll saw model.

The fact is scroll saws with low vibration are relatively expensive but incredibly worthwhile.

Blade Tensions

For most devices and tools bearing blades, the tension of the scroll saw will influence its ability to cut with precision and a level of accuracy. For instance, if your scroll saw is unable to cut straightly consistently, then your device is loose and requires tightening.

To accomplish this, you need first to review the manual. Therein lies the right information for that scroll saw model, which pieces of hardware are involved, and tools will be required to carry out the task at hand. Next, find the tension of the saw's rod and, depending on the model, make the lever located at the end of the rod tight or use a screwdriver to tighten.

From this, you can see that blade tensions are managed by tightening the lever or screw. After you must have gained control of the blade's tension, use a scrap wood to test the sharpness of the blade before you resume the project. If the tone of the blade cutting is extremely high during the test, it suggests that the tension is extremely high. On the other hand, if you get a very low tone from cutting, it is a sign the blade is still loose. Repeat the process again.

Twisted Blades

Scroll saw blades are usually designed in a wide variety of shapes, sizes, and prices. For instance, when cutting a new or unfamiliar material, it is important to have different types of blades at hand. Sometimes, you may require smaller or thinner blades to follow the woodgrain pattern of the piece of the material you wish to cut.

When the grain opposes the desired cut line, the blade can break or twist. This makes it highly difficult and almost impossible to make a clean cut. You may need to upgrade to a thicker blade or serration pattern, capable of making all the difference.

This means that if you are having challenges with twisted blades, experiment with a vast number of blade patterns and sizes.

Broken Scroll Saw Blades

Although most scroll saw blades have a short life, and you may need to replace them eventually. There are several ways to remedy frequently-broken scroll saw blades.

You need to make sure you are using the right blade. As stated earlier, using the right blade for the right wood will save you a lot of trouble. If your blades keep breaking despite this factor being in place, there are certain things you should do.

First, you need to check the tension of your blade. As you already know, too much tension or extremely low tension while you are sawing is a leading cause of scroll saw blades breaking. Using an inappropriate level of tension is a sure way to damage those blades. It will also allow you to make the wrong cuts in your wood and ultimately affect your project outcome. If you need more guidance on blade tension, you can consult No. 4 above.

Also, make sure you're approaching the woodcutting in the manner in which it should be cut. Apply the right amount of pressure for starters, and then work your way up. You don't want to put too much pressure on the saw blade, as that could be the actual reason your scroll saw is experiencing breakage.

Conduct regular checks for rust and corrosion. This doesn't just only apply to scroll saw blades, as rust can ruin the efficiency of any material. This is why you need to purchase high-quality blades. They may be quite expensive but very economical if maintained properly. Great maintenance of your tools will give them a longer shelf life.

Finally, you need to watch out for your scroll saw speed. When things are moving too fast, it's the best time to slow down. Sawdust can clog the work tool at excess speed and take things out of control. This is because when things go out of control, your blades can break.

Which end of the Blade is Top?

For some, especially beginners, it is usually not clear what end of the blade is top. If you are using a blade with a crown-tooth, it is not important because the blade cuts in either direction. When using other blades, the majority of their teeth should point downwards. To locate the tooth direction of your blade, run your thumbnail through the middle of the blade.

It appears to be rougher when you run your finger in that direction, like almost sandpaper. As soon as you locate the blade direction in one blade, ensure to apply a small dab of common red nail polish to mark the top ends of the other blades in that pack. You don't need something expensive; a cheap red polish will do.

Blades Popping out of the Blade Holders

Most manufacturers coat blades in light oil to prevent them from rusting during shipping. This oil is one of the major reasons the blade slips. To achieve this, keep good sandpaper near the saw and rub both ends of the blade with it before installing the blasé in the saw to remove the oil.

Blades also slip because the set screws that ought to hold them in place have been polished smooth over time by the action of the blade and stop gripping. A bit of sanding with good sandpaper will also help get rid of this polish and ensure the screws gain a more accurate polish.

Scorching Wood

If your blades are dull, it will surely result in friction. All forms of cutting will eventually dull the blade but cutting dense wood speeds up the process. Scorched wood is a perfect sign that the blade is getting dull and should be replaced.

Resinous wood such as cheery is sure to burn if you don't use tape or wax to lubricate the blade. Very hard wood, such as hickory, will dull blades quickly and cause scorching.

Lastly, sawdust packed into the cut will result in scorching. Try using a skip-tooth table, which removes the sawdust as it cuts.

Unmoving Blades

Let's assume you are sawing your way through the wood, cutting nice 45 degrees, and suddenly your blade stops moving. There is still power to the engine, but the blade just won't work!

When you turn it off, you can maneuver the work plate to see inside your device. It is possible that a screw came loose from inside the lower arm, which is attached to a kind of arm that is in turn attached to a plate, attached to a motor. If you reattach the loose screw and still have the same problem, you need to check the bolts.

Another possible explanation is that the bolt fell off. Check the bolt, which is meant to couple the long arm thing and the flat black thing to transfer the oscillating motion from the motor to the arm. You can't just screw it back in; first, push it past the ball bearing so that a little bit sticks out, then screw a nut back to it.

You could be missing some nuts, so head out to your local store and check out your device.

The end... almost!

Hey! We've made it to the final chapter of this book, and I hope you've enjoyed it so far.

If you have not done so yet, I would be incredibly thankful if you could take just a minute to leave a quick review on Amazon

Reviews are not easy to come by, and as an independent author with a little marketing budget, I rely on you, my readers, to leave a short review on Amazon.

Even if it is just a sentence or two!

So if you really enjoyed this book, please...

\>\> Click here to leave a brief review on Amazon.

I truly appreciate your effort to leave your review, as it truly makes a huge difference.

Chapter 6

Saw Scrolling Frequently Asked Questions (FAQs)

In this chapter, I will attempt to tackle all the possible questions regarding saw scrolling. Let's begin.

1. How does a scroll saw work?

A scroll saw is not so different from a band saw because you push the wood up against the blade to get the desired cut that you require. A band saw has a blade on a continuous loop, and the scroll saw features a reciprocating blade. It is the reciprocating blade that enables a much precise cut.

2. What can I make with a scroll saw?

A scroll saw is an indispensable tool designed for cutting frames, but it has to be a good one. Search for one with many mass to sampan vibrations, a fine variable-speed drive, and a good blade-clamping system. A used Hegner is a good investment for a start.

Another important use of scroll saw is in the cutting of intricate curves and joints, a task that can be completed more swiftly and with accuracy. The scroll saw can also be used to cut dovetail joints and are a common tool for a thicker intarsia project. When you utilize a fine blade, the kerf of a scroll saw is almost invisible.

3. Can I make money with a scroll saw?

Of course, you can make money with this impeccable wood-cutting tool. Some of the ways you can make money through saw scrolling include wooden crosses (ornately designed crosses are beautiful home decorations in any room throughout a home), name plaques, monogrammed signs.

Others include decorative boxes, topography art, wooden baskets, holiday ornaments and so much more.

4. Can I cut plywood with a scroll saw?

This selection rests with you as to whether or not you should cut plywood. Plywood possesses good tensile strength and is extremely stable. However, it will eat through your blades a little quicker than a solid softwood.

5. How is a jigsaw different from a scroll saw?

The fact is that both saw types can be used to make very curved lines and plunge cuts, the main difference is this:

a scroll saw is more precise, and a jigsaw cuts more sharply and it is also capable of doing other things well.

6. Are scroll saws dangerous?

Generally, the scroll saw is safer to use in comparison to other saws. However, if you happen to have contact with the blade during operation, you could obtain serious hand and finger injuries.

7. What is the best scroll saw blade to use?

Use blades with fewer teeth per inch (TPI) for harder, thick wood because it will cut much more aggressively. For instance, a blade with 8 TPI will certainly cut faster than a blade with 12 TPI. However, with a blade-like 12 TP1, you are sure to have major control.

8. Can you cut MDF with a scroll saw?

You can cut and make all kinds of shapes with high-grade MDF; so far, you can work with the perfect thickness between a range of ¼" and ¾". You need to note that you will require tough and sharp blades since the glue and resin in the MDF will make them blunt quickly.

9. How do you cut curves with a scroll saw?

Consider the shape and form of the pattern carefully before you head to the drill press and take note of long cuts in the piece, as well as the overall strength of the wood. This will affect your scrolling. Endeavor to plan out your cutting in advance and begin to feel closer to the center in the area you feel most likely to break; that way, if it becomes designer firewood, it happens early in the process.

If you are using a spiral, you don't need to turn the wood around the blade. Use the blade to trace the lines of the pattern making use of the entire 360 degrees of the cutting surface a spiral provides. Another technique is to change the directions while cutting.

If you feel like the cutting needs more support as you get close to completing it use clear packing tape on the top and bottom to give it some extra support. This enables you to see the pattern while giving a little strength.

10. How tight should my scroll saw be?

After tensioning and installation determine, move the scroll saw blade with your hands so that the blades should be re-tensioned. The scroll saw blade should withstand any movement when gently twisted or pushed with yours. Be very cautioned and self-conscious at this point to avoid bruises and injuries.

11. What types of wood do you use on the scroll saw?

Hardwood is the nicest and most attractive wood to use. Oakwood in varying thicknesses of ¼, ½, and ¾" thickness is usually available from large hardware stores or catalog companies like Heritage Building Specialties. A lot of people like to use walnut and mahogany for special projects. For trim, purple hearts and other exotic woods are mainly used.

Inexpensive sources of plywood like luan and fir are not so good for projects. However, high-quality Baltic birch is often used for plaques and jigsaw puzzles. Some use it for making clocks and boxes. Reasons to use Baltic birch include its inexpensiveness and its less likeliness to break.

The only downside to using plywood is that the edges aren't very attractive, but that might not be a challenge for plaques and puzzles. You need to note that glue layers in plywood will dull your blade faster than sawing the same thickness in solid wood.

When painting, plywood is highly recommended as it saves more money than using hardwood.

12. How do I keep my blade clamp from slipping?

Often, you might have trouble with the blade slipping out of the blade clamp for two reasons. This occurs mostly with the upper blade clamp and for two reasons. The first is that the interior gets very smooth, and the second is that there may be a little oil on the clamping surfaces. New blades most often have oil on them to prevent rust. And when this oil gets on the clamp, it will make the clamp slippery.

All you need to do is take a little piece of fine sandpaper and sand the inside of the clamp, just to make it a little rough. You can also clean your clamp with alcohol.

13. How do you eliminate burning?

When you use a 2" clear package tape, you can eliminate most burning, especially in wood with oil (like Purple Heart) and very hard wood. Some woodworkers like first to put the pattern on the wood and then put tape over the pattern. Others like to put it on the wood first. It all depends on you. Some might even use a different tape but most like to use the package type.

At first, it almost looks like the tape lubricates the blade. Not quite. The tape has a chemical like silicone which releases friction. If the chemical were not on top of the tape, you would never be able to unroll the tape from itself.

14. How do I estimate project time?

Some projects might require you to drill 20 holes and then cut them out. You can time yourself by how long it talks to cut the 20 holes and then multiply that by how many times you drilled 20 holes.

People would always want o to confirm the timeframe it takes for making that particular item. Make sure to attach the extra time taken for attaching the pattern, sanding, and finishing when you set your price. Cutting is only the final stage of the project. Also, don't forget overhead expenses like heating and lighting.

15. How do I cut corners?

Some people do this by spinning the wood around. This will leave around the corner. However, if you do spin the wood, make sure you stop cutting but keep your saw running. Then, turn the wood with pressure on the back of the blade so it won't remove any wood while turning.

However, you can also do this differently. There are two lines: line A going into the corner and line B going away. Cut on line A to the corner. Then, back out about a 1/4" and turn the blade with the teeth into the waste, start cutting a new curve towards the second line, line B and then to the corner. A small piece will fall out. This will give you room to turn the blade, and put the back of the blade in a corner and start cutting on line B.

16. How do I play safe when using a scroll saw?

I would say that the scroll saw is the safest woodworking tool you find. The scroll saw is a great tool for young woodworking students to learn. It cuts slowly, so there's less quick-thinking to do. Perhaps, if you ever get stuck, you can just shut off the power and relax.

That's not to say that the scroll saw cannot be dangerous because all power tools can be. All you need to do is take care. As you work with your device, remain alert and ensure you have good lighting at all times. Always don a pair of safety goggles and a mask to ensure your workspace has good ventilation.

Use the work piece guard to hold down your project firmly while still allowing it to move freely. But as you become more experiencing handling the tool, you may decide that the guard isn't necessary or that it gets in the way. If you're a beginner, though, it is always best to use a guard.

Keep your fingers away from the blade at all times and be mindful of the reciprocating arm of the scroll saw; it is responsible for most accidents in saw scrolling. However, most scroll saws come with a spring in the arm to prevent the tip from shooting down into the project or your hand when the blade breaks. Regardless, it's good to know whether your saw will react this way or not.

When a blade breaks, one end can hit your finger. You may not lose your finger but it can bleed and get blood on the fine piece of wood. While a blade won't work in hundreds of pieces, wearing safety goggles is a better way to play safe. Of course, a broken blade might hit your eye just once in hundred years, but why take the chance?

Sawdust, a by-product of your work, might be one of the greatest hazards in woodworking. Currently, scroll saw companies are changing the flow of air that blows away the dust. A good mask is one of the most protective means to avoid inhaling the dust. I also recommend an air filtration system hanging from the ceiling. This exchanges the air about 5 to 6 times every hour.

Make sure you don't have loose cords lying around. The result might be one of your new sanders and you would hate to see it fall to the floor.

Another safety tip is regarding repetitive motion injury, such as carpal tunnel syndrome. This occurs when you spend hour after hour holding down the wood on the table and can result in surgery. To avoid this, take compulsory rests for a while before resuming. Pause and stretch your hands, eyes, and wrist frequently.

17. Any tips on pricing my works?

Now, this can be quite challenging to figure out. However, you must note that a great way to stay in business is by avoiding being overpriced or underpriced.

The first thing to do is enjoy your craft. Only very few make a living from scroll sawing and woodwork. Hence, update yourself, put your work out there, attend craft shows. These should guide you on how to price your work effectively.

18. How can I remove my pattern?

Sometimes, it is possible that you wrongly place your pattern and you have to remove it to replace it or attach a new one. Here is what you need to do to make the process faster and easier for you.

Mineral spirits are miracle workers in removing paper patterns from wood surfaces.

Apply some mineral spirits on a towel and press it on the wood so that it soaks through the paper pattern and adhesive for about 15 seconds. After which, you can attempt removing the paper. All the paper would come out in one piece without shredding and leaving little pieces behind or residual glue. This is a very cheap and effective option. In case you are worried about the smell, there are odorless ones you can apply to prevent irritation.

To reuse the wood or apply wood stain, you would have to allow the wood to dry for two days so the mineral spirits can be out.

Another option is the adhesive remover.

This is a general category that includes glue is gone, paint thinner, and acetone.

Just like the mineral spirit, you would have to use a towel to apply this fluid to the wood. Allow it to soak in for a few minutes, and then instead of removing the pattern with your hands, you would have to scrub it away with the towel or another cloth. It also requires drying if you are to reuse your wood.

A third option is sanding.

You can sand off the pattern without the use of the chemical adhesive remover. This method is only effective when you have a little residual glue on the wood. It requires a little time and stress. However, you have to remove most of the paper pattern to prevent it from clogging the sandpaper.

No drying time needed, just scrub or sand off and your wood would be as good as new.

19. Why does my blade get blunt quickly?

Scroll saw blades normally last for 15-45 minutes of consistent use on any wood type at moderate speeds: the wood type, speed, and tension contribution to the lifespan of a blade.

However, experts advise that it is more important to focus on the performance of the blade than the duration it lasts. In saw scrolling, blades are meant to be consumed like sandpaper. The more effective a blade is, the faster the scrolling exercise. That way, you'll be able to get the most out of your blade in case it still goes off.

Nonetheless, to prolong the life of your blade, get the blade tension right, lubricate the blade everywhere. This helps to preserve the sharpness of the blade. Use the right texture of the material that fits your blade. Don't use hardwood with a small blade. It would destroy your blade. Also, woods with resin content could make your blade blunt because the resin sticks on the blade and if it is not cleaned out, it reduces the sharpness of the blade.

Finally, higher speed will wear your blade faster than any other thing. Practice good storage. Poor storage rustiness blades quickly.

Conclusion

An investment in the saw and other materials needed to kickstart your scrolling journey doesn't necessarily require you to break the bank; however, it is worth it if it does. To become a PRO at saw scrolling, you need to sharpen your scrolling skill by practicing more often and investing in other tools or materials that you will need in saw scrolling.

With just a little creativity, you can get exposed to many possibilities in creating lots of fun and unique designs and projects.

In this book, you have been exposed to virtually every detail you need to get you started on the right path, including how you can make profits from saw scrolling by making simple things like home décor materials and the likes. You can now have fun honing your creativity while making money with saw scrolling at the very same time. So, I implore you to take advantage of this pricey resource and keep practicing unitl you get it right and become an expert in the field in no time.

I wish you all the best. Happy scrolling, sawers!

www.ingramcontent.com/pod-product-compliance
Lightning Source LLC
Chambersburg PA
CBHW050322120526
44592CB00014B/2020